BUCKINGHAM PALACE

Introduction

Buckingham Palace is the official London residence of Her Majesty The Queen and as such is the very symbol of British sovereignty. Yet it has been in the possession of the Royal Family for only a little over 200 years.

It is also the only official Royal residence in the world which has kept a name bestowed on it by a nobleman – John Sheffield, Duke of Buckingham. Until the end of the eighteenth century, Buckingham House, which occupied the site on which Buckingham Palace now stands, was the London home of the Dukes of Buckingham. The house was bought by King George III in 1762 for £28,000, and on 22 May of the same year, His Majesty and his eighteen-year-old consort, Queen Charlotte, moved in, becoming the first Royal couple to occupy it. Strangely, it was never intended to be the principal residence of the monarch – George III bought it as a suitable home for his wife, if he should die before her. When King George IV acceded to the Throne he commissioned John Nash, the leading architect of the day, to design him 'a palace fit for a King' and much of the structure and, indeed, the decoration of Buckingham Palace as we see it today, are due to Nash and his Royal patron.

Buckingham Palace is unusual in that it is never open to the public, and even those areas which are at times accessible consist only of the State Rooms, which are used on ceremonial occasions.

Indeed, to really appreciate the splendours of the Palace and enjoy its true glories, it is necessary to be present at a State Banquet or official reception, when all the State Rooms are in use. Servants in scarlet and gold livery, ladies in full-length ballgowns, complete with sparkling diamonds and glittering tiaras and gentlemen in formal Court Dress, ceremonial uniforms or national costume, bedecked with decorations and sashes, all combine to bring to life the true brilliance of the Court. But of course, Buckingham Palace, with its 600 rooms, is far more than just the home of the Royal Family, and a place of lavish entertainment. It is also the centre of an important administrative complex, where the affairs of State are handled by an efficient, modern and intensely loyal Household, consisting of 300 men and women of widely differing talents and skills. It is here also that Her Majesty The Queen receives foreign Heads of State, leaders of the Commonwealth and representatives of the Diplomatic Corps.

It is, quite simply, the most famous address in the world.

Her Majesty The Queen and His Royal Highness The Duke of Edinburgh (opposite), *photographed by Tim Graham on the occasion of the Royal ruby wedding anniversary.*

The Royal coat of arms (left). *The shield is charged with the 'leopards' of England, the lion of Scotland and the harp of Ireland. These are the arms used by Queen Victoria and all subsequent Sovereigns. The Royal supporters are the Lion of England and the Scottish Unicorn. The shield is encircled by a blue Garter, ornamented with gold and inscribed* Honi soit qui mal y pense *(Shame on him who thinks evil of it). The Royal motto* Dieu et mon droit *(God and my right) is well known.*

An eighteenth-century view of St James's Park from Buckingham House (left) *showing the original forecourt fountain. St James's Palace can be seen, centre left, and St Paul's Cathedral, centre right.*

In 1702 an English nobleman, John Sheffield, Duke of Buckingham, commissioned the 'learned and ingenious' architect William Winde to design a mansion on the grandest site in London.

The splendid building looked down the avenue planted by King Charles II to form the Mall and was located partly on the site of the Mulberry Garden, a Royal leasehold dating from the reign of King James I when the King had experimented unsuccessfully with the French culture of silkworms. The Duke's new home was a building befitting the former Lord Chamberlain and suitor of Princess (later Queen) Anne, who had later married an illegitimate daughter of King James II.

As originally designed, Buckingham House was a brick mansion with outlying wings connected to the central block by curved colonnades. At the south end of the entrance hall a Portland stone staircase rose from an arch supported by Corinthian columns to the saloon over the hall. The walls of this staircase were painted with the story of Dido, and the ceiling, which was fifty-five feet (16.7m) from the ground, with a glorious concourse of gods and goddesses.

In front, beyond the forecourt fountain, stretched the refreshing vista which included St James's Palace on the one hand and the canal and grassy walks of St James's Park on the other. The mansion was already a focus of admiration by 1708, when the New View of London described it, prophetically, as a 'graceful palace . . . not to be contemned by the greatest monarch'.

It is said that the attention of King George III and Queen Charlotte was directed to Buckingham House by the Marquess of Carnarvon, later third Duke of Chandos, a Lord of the Bedchamber. At the time of their marriage in 1761 the lease of the Mulberry Garden was within ten years of expiry, and Sir Charles Sheffield, natural son and eventual heir of the Duke of Buckingham, having failed to obtain a renewal, sold Buckingham House to the Crown for £28,000.

The King decreed that it should be known in future as 'The Queen's House', into which the King and Queen moved on Saturday 22 May 1762.

The Grand Staircase of
Buckingham House in 1800
(above) *featured sumptuous
Baroque paintings on the walls
and ceilings depicting Dido and
Aeneas. James Wyatt's new
staircase, shown here, replaced
an earlier one by Tijou.*

The young Queen Charlotte at
her dressing-table (above right)
*with her two small sons,
George, Prince of Wales, in
Greek costume, and Prince
Frederick in Turkish robes.
A painting by Johann Zoffany,
c.1765.*

Buckingham House (below
right) *provided a neo-classic
family home for the newly
married King and Queen.
A watercolour by W. Westall
ARA, 1819.*

King George III (opposite,
above) *ordered the remarkable
Octagon Library (opposite,
below) to be built in 1768 as a
further wing to his existing
libraries, to accommodate his
vast collection of books. This
two-storeyed, galleried
apartment was one of the finest
rooms in the Palace. Dr Samuel
Johnson was a frequent visitor
to the Library.*

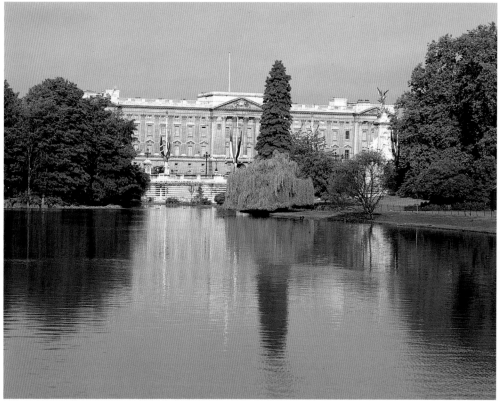

Buckingham Palace (above) *showing the Marble Arch on its original site at the entrance to the forecourt. A watercolour by Joseph Nash, 1846. This nineteenth-century view and a modern-day view* (right), *looking across the lake from St James's Park, show the Palace in its 'pastoral' setting.*

The Entrance Front (opposite below) *as first built by John Nash.*

The golden-brown Bath stone of the Garden Front (opposite, top) *with its central Bow, built by John Nash in 1825, survives almost unaltered since Georgian days. King George IV* (opposite, centre) *ordered Nash to build him a 'palace fit for a King'.*

The accession of King George IV in 1820 decided the eventual future of Buckingham House. Architects had long been dreaming of a great Royal palace, and at this period, when London was being developed in urban elegance, magnificent designs were placed before the King. He was unimpressed.

'If the public wish to have a palace,' he told his favourite architect, John Nash, 'I have no objection to build one, but I must have a pied-a-terre . . . and . . . I will have it at Buckingham House. There are early associations which endear me to the spot.' Nash was busy on his superb scheme to link Carlton House, the King's earlier home at the other end of the Mall, with Regent's Park, but in 1825 he was summoned from this absorbing task to build Buckingham Palace.

It was erected in Bath stone, and while outwardly its debt to its predecessor was barely acknowledged, at the King's desire Nash retained the shell of the earlier house and much of the plan. His Grand Hall accords with the entrance hall of Buckingham House, and the elevation of his Grand Staircase conforms in size and height to King George III's, and preserves the same form of approach to the State Rooms.

Nash added depth to the original block, and completed his new Garden Front with a semi-circular Bow in the centre and a Terrace flanked by pillared and pedimented conservatories. Along the first floor, overlooking the Royal 'pleasure grounds' laid out by William Townsend Aiton – the head gardener at Kew – he placed the Armoury at the south end, and then the apartments which are now the State Dining Room, the Blue Drawing Room, the domed Music Room in the Bow, the White Drawing Room and the Royal Closet (planned respectively as the King's State Bedchamber and Dressing Room). To divide them from the Guard Chamber, Green Drawing Room and Throne Room he designed the glass-roofed Picture Gallery, which is 155 feet (47.2m) long and 27 feet (8.2m) wide.

On the ground floor of his charming Garden Front Nash placed the Semi-State Apartments. His achievements, both inside and out, remain virtually unchanged.

7

Queen Victoria, aged eighteen, became the first Sovereign to live at Buckingham Palace. On 13 July 1837, three weeks after her accession, she drove in state from Kensington to take up residence, and the Royal Standard was raised for her on the top of the Marble Arch. Her uncle, King William IV, had died on 20 June, just as the Palace was ready for occupation.

John Nash had rightly predicted that the Palace would prove too small, but this was a fault capable of remedy. The want of a consecrated chapel was filled after the Queen's marriage to Prince Albert of Saxe-Coburg and Gotha, the south conservatory being made into one in 1843.

In 1847 the architect Edward Blore added the East Front, which is pierced with a central and two lateral archways and has at the south end the Visitors' Entrance and at the north the Privy Purse Entrance. Along the first floor he placed the Principal Corridor, a gallery 240 feet (73.1m) long overlooking the Quadrangle and divided into three sections by folding doors of mirror glass. It links the Royal Corridor on the north with the Household Corridor on the south, and opens into suites of semi-state rooms facing the

State Ball at Buckingham Palace (above), 5 July 1848. Eugene Lami's watercolour shows Nash's Grand Staircase of the late 1820s in its full glory.

The East Front of Buckingham Palace (left) in 1847, showing the Privy Purse Entrance on the right. The ornate gateways and railings were not erected around the Palace forecourt until 1906 when the Queen Victoria Memorial was also begun.

Queen Victoria (right) *and her Consort, Prince Albert, dressed as Queen Philippa and King Edward III. Sir Edwin Landseer's painting of the Royal couple suggests the sumptuous grandeur of the great costume balls held in the Palace during Victoria's reign – their splendour was talked about for decades.*

The Ballroom at Buckingham Palace (below), *17 June 1856. Queen Victoria commissioned this magnificent room to be built in 1854. It is the largest in the Palace, measuring more than 120 feet (36.5m) long by 60 feet (18m) wide. In this watercolour by Louis Haghe, the Queen can be seen seated on the Throne at the west end.*

Mall and St James's Park. Blore introduced into the East Front some of the finest fittings from George IV's Royal Pavilion at Brighton, which Queen Victoria ceased to use after the purchase of Osborne House.

The new building rendered the Marble Arch both functionally and ornamentally dispensable, and it was removed in 1850 to its present site at the north-east corner of Hyde Park.

Only one important structural addition remained to be made. In 1854 Sir James Pennethorne, pupil of John Nash, removed the Armoury and the Octagon Library of King George III and erected a Ballroom 123 feet (37.4m) long and 60 feet (18.2m) wide, with a throne dais at the west end and an organ and musicians' gallery at the other. Below it he placed spacious kitchens.

Mars and Venus (above), *a marble group by the Italian sculptor Antonio Canova (1757–1822) commissioned by King George IV after Canova's visit to England in 1815.*

The Grand Hall (below).

The principal floor of Buckingham Palace is the first floor, which is where most of the magnificent State Rooms are located. It is reached via the Grand Entrance which is only visible from the front of the Palace through the main arch, as it dates from the time when the Palace was built around only three sides of the Quadrangle.

The coupled columns which surround the Grand Hall are each composed of a single block of veined Carrara marble enriched with Corinthian capitals of gilded bronze.

The Grand Staircase, designed by John Nash in 1825, leads from the Grand Hall to the first floor. It is a truly superb construction, the marble steps dividing into three flights at the first landing, two flights curving upward to right and left and meeting before the marble doorway into the Guard Room, the third section carrying on to the East Gallery.

The Guard Room, containing a number of marble statues, is the ceremonial entrance to the Green Drawing Room.

The Guard Room (above), *containing a number of marble statues, the finest being of Prince Albert.*

The Grand Staircase (opposite).

*The Green Drawing Room
(below),* looking towards the
Picture Gallery.

The Green Drawing Room, the first of the State Rooms, is the central apartment on the west side of the Quadrangle. It has three windows opening on to the loggia over the Grand Entrance and three corresponding mirror-doors leading to the Picture Gallery. The elegant Green Drawing Room is aptly named as the chairs and sofas are all upholstered in green silk and the walls are hung with brocade of the same colour. The colours are soft and muted. The off-white and gold of the pilasters and ceiling complement the deep crimson and gold of the Axminster carpet. The furniture includes two late eighteenth-century French ebony-veneered cabinets.

Guests at Royal functions enter the Green Drawing Room before any of the other State Rooms and they pass through one of the mirrored doors into the Picture Gallery.

*French cabinet panel detail,
eighteenth century* (left). *Sèvres
vase, 1758* (above).

*The Green Drawing Room
(opposite),* view towards the
loggia.

Chinese-style black Sèvres porcelain vase (above), *c.1790, decorated with* chinoiserie *scenes in platinum and gold.*

The Picture Gallery (below).

In the early days of Queen Victoria's reign, State Banquets were held in the Picture Gallery but when the new State Ballroom was completed in the 1850s, the Queen decided that the Ballroom was a more suitable setting and the Picture Gallery reverted to its original use. It owes much of its present excellent condition to Queen Mary, who made many improvements during the reign of her husband King George V. Her Majesty installed new lighting, had the number of pictures greatly reduced and replaced the original crimson carpet with several multi-coloured rugs which lend the gallery a more restful air.

The State Dining Room is used for formal meals which are not quite as grand as State Banquets. It is an elegant room, dominated by a portrait of King George IV in his coronation robes, who looks down on a massive mahogany dining table.

Mounted Japanese lacquer bowl (above), *early eighteenth century.*

The Picture Gallery in 1843 (right), a watercolour by D. Morison, which shows the paintings displayed in bewildering profusion, before Queen Mary's improvements were introduced.

The State Dining Room (below).

Sèvres vase (below), *c.1770, acquired by King George IV in 1829.*

The Blue Drawing Room (above).

The Music Room (opposite).

Detail from the 'Table of the Grand Commanders' (below), a gift to King George IV from Louis XVIII.

One of the most beautiful rooms in Buckingham Palace is the Blue Drawing Room, a lofty apartment whose richly carved ceiling is supported by columns printed in imitation onyx. The room is illuminated by four magnificent crystal chandeliers from which the light sparkles and shimmers on to the heavy silk curtains and exquisite gilt chairs, all in the coolest shade of ice blue. The Axminster carpet is predominantly red in colour but the blue from which the room takes its name is cleverly woven into the intricate pattern.

The magnificent Music Room is one of the State Apartments which has retained its character practically unchanged since the days of Queen Victoria. In modern times the Music Room has become the setting for Royal christenings and where guests are presented at State Visits – though the room still contains a grand piano.

Mosaic jewel egg by Fabergé (above), *revealing portraits of the five Russian Imperial children.*

The White Drawing Room (opposite).

The White Drawing Room is the most glittering of the State Rooms. Its walls are painted white and gold but the predominant colour is pale yellow. The furniture is upholstered in yellow damask and the colour is dramatically reflected by the giant twelve-feet (3.7m) high mirror doors which open immediately on to the Picture Gallery.

The most dramatic feature of this room is the mirror in one corner which, at first sight, gives no indication of being anything out of the ordinary. However, at State functions it swings open silently, and apparently at the touch of a button, to reveal the Royal Family, who appear before their guests.

The State Ballroom is used only rarely for dancing these days, its main function being the setting for the State Banquets held for visiting Heads of State or, more frequently, for Investitures. The crimson canopy at one end of the room was designed by Lutyens and first used in India for King George V's Coronation Durbar, held in 1911.

A pair of silver gilt crab salts and spoons (above), *one of several exquisite decorations which adorn the State banqueting table.*

The State Ballroom (below).

The State Rooms

One of the main State Rooms is the Throne Room, the setting for the wedding group photographs of the Duke and Duchess of York in July 1986. The beautiful ornamented ceiling is acknowledged to be one of the finest examples of early nineteenth-century craftsmanship, which is cleverly illuminated by the seven crystal chandeliers whose candles were replaced by electric light bulbs in 1901.

The frieze, which depicts scenes from the Wars of the Roses, dates from the reign of William IV. Standing on the dais under the canopy are the Throne chairs of Her Majesty the Queen and the Duke of Edinburgh. On either side of the Throne dais the wall is ornamented with carved and gilt trophies by Henry Holland, said to have come from the Throne Room at Carlton House, the former home of King George IV.

The beautiful garlanded sculptures under the beam in front of the Throne dais depict winged Victories and are by Bernasconi.

The Throne Room (below), *looking to the Green Drawing Room, with the Guard Room and Grand Staircase beyond.*

The Throne Room (right).

Buckingham Palace may well be the most famous building in the world and is known to millions of visitors as The Queen's home, yet it is only the principal official residence of the Sovereign.

Although Her Majesty spends much of the working year in residence, only a tiny proportion of the Palace's 600 rooms are occupied by the Royal Family and only a handful of the 300 men and women who work there come into regular contact with The Queen.

The Palace is very much a working building; the centre of a large office complex which is necessary for the complicated and extensive administration of the modern monarchy. The seat of Royal administration is still St James's Palace, and foreign ambassadors are officially accredited to the Court of St James's, even though the ceremony when the envoys officially present Letters of Credence to The Queen actually takes place at Buckingham Palace. The proclamation of a new Sovereign continues to take place at St James's Palace.

Inside Buckingham Palace are a Post Office and a police station; staff canteens and Household Dining Rooms. The kitchens sometimes serve up to 600 meals a day and the Post Office deals with over 100,000 items every year. There is a special three-man security team equipped with a fluoroscope, which examines every piece of mail that arrives at the Palace.

There is also a soldier who is responsible for making sure the Royal Standard is flying whenever The Queen is in residence, and to make sure it is taken down when she leaves. It is his job to watch for the moment when the Royal limousine turns into the Palace gates – at the very second The Queen enters her Palace, the Royal Standard is hoisted.

Buckingham Palace is not only the home of the Royal Family but also the workplace of an army of secretaries, clerks and typists, telephonists, carpenters and plumbers. There are gardeners, chauffeurs and coachmen in the Royal Mews, upholsterers and seamstresses, mechanics and engineers, cooks, kitchen hands, footmen, butlers, stewards, maids and cleaners, policemen and soldiers, and

The Centre Room · The Carnarvon Room

The Centre Room (right), *from which members of the Royal Family emerge* (above), *to wave from the balcony to the crowds, after ceremonial occasions.*

An honour is conferred in the State Ballroom (opposite, above) *by Prince Charles. Fourteen Investitures are held annually when men and women, watched by their families, receive awards for public service.*

Visiting Heads of State assemble in the Music Room (opposite, centre) *before a State Banquet in the Ballroom. Her Majesty The Queen and Her Majesty Queen Elizabeth The Queen Mother are seen with The Duke of Edinburgh and the President of Nigeria and his wife.*

The Carnarvon Room (opposite, below), *part of the Belgian Suite, which is used to accommodate visiting Heads of State.*

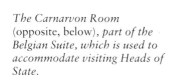

two men belonging to the Royal Collection Department who wind and maintain the Palace's 300 clocks.

The business of monarchy never stops and the light is often shining from the window of The Queen's study late at night as she works on the famous 'boxes', the red and blue leather cases in which are delivered the State papers, official letters and reports which follow her wherever she is in the world.

All the offices of those closest to Her Majesty – her Private Secretaries – are located on the ground floor corridor immediately beneath her private apartments. Visitors enter the Palace by the Privy Purse Door, on the extreme right as you look at the building from the Mall.

The senior member of The Royal Household is the Lord Chamberlain. He has a wide variety of responsibilities, including all ceremonial duties relating to the Sovereign, apart from the wedding, coronation and funeral of a monarch, which remain the responsibility of the Earl Marshal, the Duke of Norfolk.

23

There are six main departments at Buckingham Palace: the Private Secretary's Office; the Privy Purse and Office of Treasurer to The Queen; the Master of the Household's Department; the Royal Mews; the Lord Chamberlain's Office, and the Royal Collection Department. The Private Secretary is The Queen's closest aide and looks after all her official correspondence and programme of events. The Press Office also comes under his control. The Keeper of the Privy Purse looks after the finances of the Royal Household and he also acts as Treasurer to the Sovereign for both personal and public accounts.

There are more than 200 domestic staff employed at Buckingham Palace and each one comes under the jurisdiction of the Master of the Household. With more

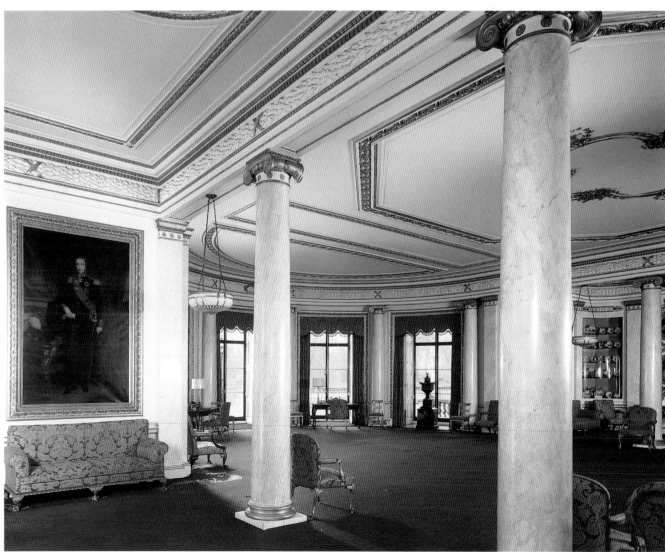

The Queen's Audience Room (right), *one of Her Majesty's rooms in the private suite along the first floor of the West Front, which overlooks the Palace gardens.*

The 1844 Room (opposite, above), *commemorates the first State Visit in that year by Tsar Nicholas I. The room is favoured by The Queen and The Duke of Edinburgh for their private luncheon parties.*

The Bow Room (opposite, below), *best-known to the outside world, as guests at Royal Garden Parties pass through its glass doors to reach the Terrace.*

A brougham from the Royal Mews *delivers letters and packages to certain central London offices each day.*

than eighty functions held in the Palace each year, ranging from the small informal luncheons given by The Queen to the three annual Garden Parties, to each of which some 9,000 guests are invited, the job of controlling the many domestic departments within the Royal Household is a demanding one.

The Queen is without doubt the world's most generous host and during any one year as many as 30,000 guests will be invited to one of the many functions. There are at least two State Banquets when 170 guests join Her Majesty in the State Ballroom (see page 19) to honour a visiting Head of State. The Ballroom is also used regularly for the fourteen Investitures which are held every year, at each of which 150 men and women are given awards personally for public service, watched by members of their families. Once a year, in November, a reception is held for members of the Diplomatic Corps in London, when 1,200 guests from nearly every country in the world turn up wearing full Court Dress, ceremonial uniforms or national costume. It is regarded as the most splendid social occasion of the year and invitations are highly prized.

The Crown Equerry runs the Royal Mews (see page 27) and is responsible for all Royal travel on land, whether by car, State Coach or on horseback. The Royal Family has an enviable record for being on time; the responsibility for maintaining it rests with the Crown Equerry.

The Lord Chamberlain's Office has the widest variety of responsibilities. It looks after all incoming visits by overseas Heads of State, the administration of the Chapels Royal and the cleaning of the Crown Jewels. It also supervises the appointment of Pages of Honour (the boys who attend the Sovereign on State occasions), the Sergeants at Arms, the Marshal of the Diplomatic Corps, the Master of The Queen's Music, the Keeper of the Jewel House at the Tower of London, the Poet Laureate, the Royal Bargemaster and the Keeper of The Queen's Swans.

The Garden Party Office is part of the Lord Chamberlain's Office and is manned by a group of temporary lady clerks who write out in longhand each of the many invitations that are despatched in Her Majesty's name.

The Director of the Royal Collection is responsible for what is arguably the most valuable private collection of works of art in the world, all of which is meticulously catalogued and perfectly maintained.

The Palace Gardens

The nearly forty acres of Buckingham Palace's gardens provide a peaceful oasis for the Royal Family in the heart of London. They form the largest private garden in the capital.

The formal gardens of the original Buckingham House were laid out to the design of Henry Wise on the orders of the Duke of Buckingham at a cost of £1,000 and included a canal 600 yards (548.6m) long, lined on either side with avenues of lime trees. When George IV built his palace he engaged William Townsend Aiton to landscape the grounds, leaving little of Wise's formal arrangements. The canal was filled in to make part of the vast, sweeping lawns and two existing ponds were joined together to form the present lake which extends to four acres, and where, since 1961, a flock of exotic, pink flamingoes have made their home.

When Her Majesty The Queen's father King George VI came to the Throne in 1936, his Consort (now Queen Elizabeth the Queen Mother, who is still recognised as one of the most avid Royal gardeners) swept away the dense Victorian shrubs and bushes and replaced them with a variety of lighter foliage and decorative flowering trees. These give the garden a delightful atmosphere of informality, at the same time providing a sense of privacy.

The Royal Garden Parties (above), when thousands of guests throng the Palace lawns, represent Royal hospitality on a grand scale.

The picturesque and fantastic Garden Pavilion (above, left), which graced the lakeside until 1928, when it was demolished.

The rose garden (left), view of the North-West Conservatory and the Garden Front.

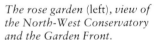

The Waterloo Vase (above), on the North Lawn, stands 15 feet (4.5m) high and is carved out of a single piece of marble. It was presented to King George IV after Waterloo.

The herbaceous border (left), fully 175 yards (160m) long, is one of the garden's true glories.

The Royal Mews

Royal coachman (above) in Full State livery, consisting of a scarlet and gold frock-coat with scarlet knee-breeches, white silk stockings, gold buckled shoes and a wig and tricorne hat.

Whenever The Queen travels by road, whether by Royal limousine, State carriage or on horseback, the responsibility for making all the necessary arrangements rests with the Crown Equerry, the man who is in charge of the Royal Mews.

The titular head of the Royal Mews is the Master of the Horse, one of the Great Officers of the Royal Household who ranks third in the order of precedence at Court, behind the Lord Great Chamberlain and the Lord Steward. In former days the Master of the Horse actually had day-to-day charge of the Royal Mews but today his duties are purely ceremonial. In State processions he can be seen riding immediately behind the Sovereign.

The Royal Mews at Buckingham Palace dates from 1825 and the buildings are still largely unchanged from Nash's original design for King George IV. The Mews is constructed around a quadrangle, with the east side reserved for the State coaches and carriages and the horses stabled on the north and west sides. There are thirty of these: the bays which are used every day, and the famous Windsor Greys which pull The Queen's coach on ceremonial occasions.

The garages contain the five Rolls-Royce limousines belonging to The Queen, the most famous of which is the Phantom VI presented to Her Majesty in March 1978 by the Society of Motor Manufacturers and Traders to mark the Silver Jubilee, the year before.

The pride of the Royal Mews is undoubtedly the magnificent collection of historic State Coaches. The most famous of them all is the gold State Coach, built in 1762, and used at every coronation since that of King George IV.

The most frequently seen is the Australian State Coach, which is used to convey The Queen to the State Opening of Parliament. This is the most recent addition to the Mews, a gift from the people of Australia during the country's Bicentennial year of 1988.

The most comfortable of the three major State Coaches is the Scottish State Coach, favoured by Queen Elizabeth the Queen Mother, with its large windows and glass panels in the roof. Visitors to the Royal Mews are also able to see the beautiful Glass Coach, used by every Royal bride this century for the drive to her marriage.

The collection of State Coaches, landaus and carriages is complemented by a fascinating exhibition of State harness, together with many photographs and other items of historical interest.

The gilded State Coach (right), famed above all others and coach detail (below). The State Coach was used for The Queen's coronation, and every coronation since the reign of King George IV.

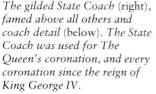

There are more than 5,000 paintings in The Royal Collection apart from countless other important works of art: sculptures, furniture, wood carvings, the Fabergé collection, exquisite porcelain and china, intricate pieces of silver and gold, valuable antique books and documents, the priceless carpets and literally thousands of private family photographs.

Each and every one of these precious objects is the responsibility of the Director of the Royal Collection, who works from an office in St James's Palace. His is an awesome task, for it is freely acknowledged that if all the items in The Royal Collection were to be assembled in a single building, they would constitute one of the most important museums.

The Queen, recognising that it is equally important for members of the public to be able to see her treasures from time to time, has made a unique contribution to the world of art by creating her own gallery in which exhibitions are held throughout the year.

Treasures from the Royal Collection on show in the Queen's Gallery (above), extending a share in Her Majesty's heritage to the world at large. This unique public art gallery was erected on the ruins of the private Royal chapel, bombed during the Second World War.